UGLY DUCKLING PRESSE
Eastern European Poets Series #23

THE LIFE AND OPINIONS OF DJ SPINOZA
© EUGENE OSTASHEVSKY 2008

EASTERN EUROPEAN POETS SERIES #23
SERIES EDITOR: MATVEI YANKELEVICH
ASSOCIATE EDITOR: GENYA TUROVSKAYA
GUEST EDITOR: ANNA MOSCHOVAKIS

THIS BOOK WAS MADE POSSIBLE IN PART BY A GENEROUS GRANT FROM THE NATIONAL ENDOWMENT
FOR THE ARTS AND CONTINUING SUPPORT FROM THE NEW YORK STATE COUNCIL ON THE ARTS,
A STATE AGENCY.

CATALOGING-IN-PUBLICATION DATA IS AVAILABLE FROM THE LIBRARY OF CONGRESS

DISTRIBUTED TO THE TRADE AS ISBN-13: 978-1-933254-44-9
BY SPD (SMALL PRESS DISTRIBUTION)
1341 SEVENTH STREET, BERKELEY, CA 94710
WWW.SPDBOOKS.ORG

DISTRIBUTED TO THE TRADE AS ISBN-13: 978-0-981552-10-1
BY CONSORTIUM BOOK DISTRIBUTION
(THROUGH AN ARRANGEMENT WITH ZEPHYR PRESS)
WWW.CBSD.COM

AVAILABLE DIRECTLY FROM UDP
AND THROUGH OUR PARTNER BOOKSTORES

FIRST EDITION 2008
PRINTED IN THE USA

UGLY DUCKLING PRESSE
THE OLD AMERICAN CAN FACTORY
232 THIRD STREET #E002
BROOKLYN NY 11215

WWW.UGLYDUCKLINGPRESSE.ORG

State of the Arts

NYSCA

NATIONAL
ENDOWMENT
FOR THE ARTS
A great nation
deserves great art.

THE LIFE AND OPINIONS OF DJ SPINOZA

EUGENE OSTASHEVSKY

DRAWINGS BY EUGENE TIMERMAN

THE LIFE AND OPINIONS OF DJ SPINOZA

EUGENE OSTASHEVSKY

Perfect were his members beyond comprehension...
Unsuited for understanding, difficult to perceive.
Four were his eyes.

—*The Enuma Elish*

Language is the first compromise we make.

—Eugene Timerman

TABLE OF DISCONTENTS

1.
She circles inside
the proof of the axiom

The axiom is self-evident
Is it true

2.
Is a wavelength blue
Is a wave a wave

She performs a gesture
with her hand

3.
If she hit rock
she could build a house

If she built a house
she could look out of the window

4.
O, no! There's an axiom
inside the proof of the axiom

and another
and another

5.
She cannot tell
the net from the knot

fact from effect
All, as Parmenides says, is one

6.
She walks in woe
from lodgment to lodgment

trying to make
an analytic judgment

The hearing
daughter of the deaf

dreams aloud
in Sign

In French
she is *la fille des sourds*

She has
a Dedekind Cut

She says: / t / / k / / p /
mutter babble

Her first words
are not in her Muttersprache

She walks
cries mutter

mutter mutter
Die Mutter kann nicht hören

The mother is crushed
between the sides of her bed

Why
It is because they are so many

the dead

He walks around walks around
DJ Spinoza

He looks like a circle
from which sticks out a snorkel

He says, Hey Flipper
You're next in line

for the French throne!
For your directions aren't overthrown

by th' element they swim in
You almost talk

whereas I sit under infinitesimal pieces of glass
instead of doing philosophy

If I were a rich man
all day I would tiddi-tiddi-dum

for the order of tiddi-tiddi-dum
repeats the order of things

I know
it is so

Look,
> A cow flies
> A fly cows
>
> A rat larks
> A lark rats
>
> But a dog dogs
> A bug bugs

All sorts of things are happening
in the bayou

The Begriffon
is something out of Geistesgeschichte

but then so is DJ Spinoza
They gather

in an obscure region of the Little Magellan Cloud
on a rock abandoned by Mr. Clam

The Begriffon looks like
$$\frac{x^2}{a^2} - \frac{y^2}{b^2} = 1$$

His eyes may be mistaken
for his nose

He can't stand
lying

The front of his T-shirt says
I AM AMBIVALENT

The back of his T-shirt says
I AM NOT AMBIVALENT

When he gets irascible
he is not very erasable

because he has 2.7×10^5 claws
but he can't find his one pair of clippers!

DJ Spinoza is misleadingly cuddly
His instructions say, HANDLE WITH CARE

On a periodic table
he lays out his definitions
                axioms
                propositions
like dentist's tools before drilling a cavity

And then they begin to fight!

The Begriffon shows the DJ three fingers
but the DJ shows the Begriffon *four* fingers

The Begriffon makes a face
but the DJ already has one

DJ Spinoza picks up a fiddle
and plays the Ditty of the Excluded Middle

The Begriffon stiffens his feet and hands
and cries, I won't dance,

merci beaucoup!
De rien, says DJ Spinoza

The Begriffon flies at him with a shriek
of whaddayamean's (cause the DJ can't stand 'em)

but the DJ replies with a double drop-kick
and follows it up with a *quod erat demonstrandum*

The Begriffon folds like a memorandum
Has he lost the will to fight?!
Find out in the second half of this poem!

THE SECOND HALF OF THIS POEM

DJ Spinoza towers over the rock
The Begriffon takes a walk around the mental block

DJ Spinoza swings a chain
of syllogisms

The Begriffon objects
to the absence of symbolism

and then—like a matching-funds grant application—
challenges the foundation

He puts his best foot forward and says:

Listen DJ Spinoza I had enough of your logocentrism
Words are justifications only

Only physical power
adjudicates the quizzical hour

Only the fist
differentiates between resist and desist

Have you ever seen giraffes
hold a symposium?

The consciousness of animals is pure time
untrammeled by the vagaries of *Sic probo*

Let us meet man to man
in the style of the whooping crane

or the praying mantis
Let us dismiss words

in toto
as the unionized janitors of reality!

DJ Spinoza replies:

Listen you, чудо-юдо заморский Begriffon
I don't care for your praying mantis
            your whooping crane
            eagle or monkey

For I shall kick your arse
    with the only style I know
    a style unabashedly virile
    in its simplicity

I shall do it
more geometrico!

wha
huang
boomsie
loop

The Begriffon stands for me, Eugene Ostashevsky
so naturally he is victorious

Sortes says to Aial:
Your axioms

contradict each other
You do not know this

Let me show it to you
What is the Good

Describe
on two double-spaced pages

in twelve-point font
Use only nouns

or rather no words
at all, we've had enough of those

I cannot see,
Aial makes to say

but instead says: Baaa
              Moo
              Bow wow

The Laughing Philosopher has entered
the Witless Relocation Program

Outside his window there's a rooster
that looks like a toaster

In the field there's a cow
on whose rump sits a crow

The crow snaps its wings, caws erratically
but the cow only smiles enigmatically

The Laughing Philosopher thinks,
Ah Nature

nonexistent daughter
of the rhetoric of cognition

We cannot reach you
But there are your representatives

speechless, the animals
conscious machines

of self-replicating nucleic acids
What is life Nature

How does it appear
by accident

How does it stand
on its own four feet

What does it see
out of the moist convexity of its eye

In a city emptied by bombs
walks DJ Spinoza

He says, I have defeated
the second argument

Man
is not a substance

Nor woman, tree
street, tower

They aren't
self-caused

Their essence
does not imply existence

I have defeated
the second argument

I have defeated
the second argument

He walks into a bar
with the Laughing Philosopher and the Weeping Philosopher

The Laughing Philosopher can't speak—
he's laughing

The Weeping Philosopher can't speak—
he's weeping

But not DJ Spinoza
DJ Spinoza sails in a sub

named *Specie Aeternitatis*
early in the morning!

He speaks, I have invented
a language for depicting the real

My language consists of the one element A
for God alone
                    is real

The fact that I can think of him
means he exists

All other things lack this property
This is why
                    they vanish

because they aren't self-caused
He is their cause

He is their substance
He is what they are

Therefore I shall represent them accordingly:

AAAAAAAAAAA

                              AAAA

             AAAAAAAAAAAAAAAAA

           AAAAAAA

Clouds move over DJ Spinoza
What are they like

They are not like anything
not even clouds

DJ Spinoza looks at the clouds
with eyes ruined

by the cutting of lenses
The clouds are blurry

Clouds, thinks DJ Spinoza,
belong to the class of things

that are not like anything
In this they are like love

What do you know about love
DJ Spinoza, you lead

a life among furniture
You call this life

You call this furniture
The question dictates the answer

The answer dictates the question
Language

1.

Wer reitet so spät durch Nacht und Wind?
Es ist DJ Spinoza!

2.

There is no justification by doubt,
thinks DJ Spinoza,

because there is no justification
and no non-justification.

3.

I read *The Guide for the Perplexed*,
says DJ Spinoza,
and it didn't work.

4. THE PARABLE OF THE ROCK

A rock flies in the direction of Cratylus. Cratylus does not move, because: what is rock? what is flies? what is Cratylus? The rock hits DJ Spinoza.

A rock flies in the direction of DJ Spinoza. DJ Spinoza does not move, because: what is rock? what is flies? what is DJ Spinoza? The rock hits DJ Spinoza.

5.

DJ Spinoza challenges Cratylus to a duel. Cratylus doesn't show.
DJ Spinoza stands in the summer heat, wondering who won.

The formula for the existence of DJ Spinoza
cannot be demonstrated within the bounds of this calculus.

Luckily, the formula for the non-existence of DJ Spinoza
cannot be demonstrated within this calculus either.

Whew! That was a close call,
thinks DJ Spinoza.

DJ Spinoza runs
among thoughts of women

He says to Roland, Sire
There's been a grave error

Those you fought were Basques
fiercely independent

admirers of modern art
more European than Goethe

They mined your horse
and it blew up when you jumped in the saddle

I should have known they were Basques,
    Roland says to DJ Spinoza
By the looks of their casques

By the widths of their masks
I should have known they were Basques

And when they unfurled
those postcolonial soccer scarves

then I *definitely* should have known they were Basques
That's who hit us with rocks

without so much as an apology
And to think we gave them electricity and archeology

Put down that horn, Laurence Olivier
It won't bring back Western civilization

AOI

DJ Spinoza says to Roland, Sire
There's been a grave error

You've caused them a lot of suffering,
your schoolmasters

Alcuin, first ever minister of culture
Hrabanus Maurus, lover of number theory

and Fridugis of Tours
with his dumb-ass Boethian semiotics

France has got the yearning for the learning
Even the emperor keeps letter blocks under his pillow

because he dreams of one day waking up literate
whereas you… you…

Blow that horn, Laurence Olivier
as a manly dirge for *la mission civilizatrice*

Roland says to DJ Spinoza
        Okay, so we fought the wrong people
What do you want me to do:

smash my sword because of it
next to where my buddy lies dying

(Laurence Olivier)
from 153 slash 'n' stab wounds

got by running through a glass pane
at the new museum

because I mistook it for a mosque
dedicated to "Mr. Apollo"?

There's so many wars to come on this continent
Who cares what happened in this one

Olivier, can you hear me? I said: Put down that horn
Our deeds will be recorded in minuscule

AOI

DJ Spinoza and MC Squared
reason on reason

Ug marug, says DJ Spinoza
Blatz kegeretz, replies MC Squared

Take 17 knights, proposes DJ Spinoza
riding in search of criminal activity

Are they lost in nature
or nurture?

Is that a grin behind their grille
or a grimace that they are ill^e?

And how shall they ever achieve enlightenment?
¡Ai, pappi!

DJ Spinoza and MC Squared
stand in an ideogrammatic landscape

composed by 1000 creative writing students
with dog-hair brushes

There's air
and there are turrets
and there's a nymph in the river

On a hilltop two Jews
argue about the ruse
of the infinitely large hypotenuse

What are my axioms
cries DJ Spinoza

but that which is self-evident to all men
The angels' banquet, sappers of doubt

the banishers of the language game
I have assembled an armature of adamant glass

which the many will consume from without
and then from within: like cud

And they shall ascend
towards sure and certain knowledge

of ontology and consequently morality
This murderer is 76% in the wrong

These tanks have 35% reason to be in this square
The hysteria of this historian is 83% histrionic

O MC Squared, the rose I clutch is only 62% alive
and my relationship with my parents is only 57% of what it
      should be

Tell me, MC Squared
If morality is deduced from mortality

and t stands for time
what time is it with you, MC Squared?

It is $\displaystyle\sum_{n=1}^{\infty} n^2$

says MC Squared

DJ Spinoza storms off
breaking into a defiant song:

Well, some philosophers wake up one morning with a big L
   on their forehead, standing for LOSER
but that never happened to DJ Spinoza!

And some philosophers return to the shtetl and marry a girl
   named Rosa
but that never happened to DJ Spinoza!

Dear Owl
you have big eyes

feathers that stick in all different directions
you wake up

your panties are funny
You hear

the sounds words make
as they plead for life

that's all that remains
of the language of language

O Owl
among leaves

what is this forest
of "letters," black light

of unintelligible suns
I cannot see

who I am
who you are

the difference between good and evil
the end of human desire

how to tell the truth
and why

Is this my life
Are you in it

for Dario

The mathematician's father says to the mathematician:
"My daughter, cars are special among objects of cognition
Because when you get in and turn on the ignition
Nothing happens (you discover) and you go call the auto mechanic

Who brings a little human warmth into your world.
So string passion fruit and apricots from the rafters of your vehicle,
Plant a pomegranate tree in place of the antenna and populate it
    with songbirds,
For it is not every day a little human warmth comes into our world."

The auto mechanic's mother says to the auto mechanic:
"My son, consider the meaning of instruments—adjustable wrench,
    monkey wrench, Allen wrench,
Mandolin, lute, recorder, electric drill—
They facilitate the transformation of nature into artifact by means
    of labor

And everything has an end, including labor,
And what is the end of labor? *Nu*, you don't know? I didn't think
    you would. You're stupid, my son. That's why you're an auto
    mechanic. Love!
Love is like a well-chosen simile:
It fills both of its members with another and shared light."

The auto mechanic says to the mathematician:
"Did you ever see spaghetti stick to each other in hot water?

And turtles lay eggs although weeping tears as big as the
    shipwreck of the *Medusa*
While doing so?

Let us break ground for gardens and academias,
Let arts and letters flourish in our private empire as only arts
    and letters can do!
Lo, I envision an aviary full of scholastic parrots ('*Hic*' and '*hoc*,'
    '*quid*' and '*ut dixit*').
Where is my National Audubon Guide to Fourteenth-Century
    Philosophers of Language?"

The mathematician says to the auto mechanic:
"Aristotle in an uncharacteristic moment
Calls mathematics the study of beauty.
Of series divergent and convergent, only the convergent can
    serve as the foundation of number.

Stand you in my neighborhood, auto mechanic.
Let arts and letters flourish in our private empire as only arts
    and letters can do.
I feel my breasts swelling already
For it is not every day a little human warmth comes into our
    world."

I used to be a curious toy,
       says Che Bourashka
I used to be an anonymous toy
and no one ever said, "Hey,
                       What's happening, baby!
How about it, me and you?" No, no one.

When I killed the emperor of China
by a fusillade of thumbtacks
at the opening of a junior high school in Guangzhou,
who was there to admire it?

When I facilitated the revolution in Mauritania
by sticking chewing gum
down riflebarrels in the Arsenal of the Mauritanian Secret Service
(a job that took many a lonely night spent in chewing!),
who was there to share my victory with me?

And who would have heard my inspirational talk
as I perished with my eyes blazing
under a hail of bullets
in the moist jungles of Bulimia?
So I married a crocodile—did I have any other choice?

Enter Creative Writing Student.

CREATIVE WRITING STUDENT: Wow!

CHE: What 'wow'?

STUD: Did I hear you right? You said you married a crocodile. Wow! What was that *like*?

CHE: Well, the size of that thing...

STUD: I'm not sure I want to hear this!

CHE: ...when he lay there all day in the bathtub with his tail sticking out! And the birds!

STUD: What birds?

CHE: The birds that came every day to lunch on the food particles he had stuck in his teeth! Disgusting! The whole apartment speckled with birdshit! And who do you think cleaned it up? He cleaned it up? I cleaned it up—on my knees, every evening...

STUD: I'm sorry to hear it... Do you know any editors?

CHE: And his birthday—do you know what happened on his birthday?

STUD: No. What happened on his birthday?

CHE: He swallowed the whole cake! At once! And then he swallowed the table! the loveseat! the TV!—and then he looks me that look, you know, I barely made it to the bathroom. So he hurls himself at the door—over and over and over!—and he's screaming, "I'm gonna get you, you hairy-eared son of a bitch!"

STUD: Sounds awful.

CHE: Awful? The fright of my life! How the hook shook in that—whatchamacallit, the metal doodad that the hook goes into?

STUD: I don't know.

CHE: Well, that—doodad! How the hook shook in it, I still can't get it out of my head: the doodad going to and fro and I just know it'll fly out of the doorframe in the next couple of seconds and—

STUD: And?

CHE: And—Blamm! I wake up and I realize: I'm not by the bathroom door, I'm on my bedroom floor; I'm no Che Bourashka, I'm MC Squared; and this is no crocodile, it's... Wait! Wait! Are you?? DJ Spinoza!

DJ SPINOZA (*unmasking himself*): El Cabron! I have you at last!

They fight. Che Bourashka is slain.

DJ SPINOZA (*triumphantly*): Gamaiù!
                          Badabà!

Lumakidù!
Breks! breks!

Exit with body. Drums.

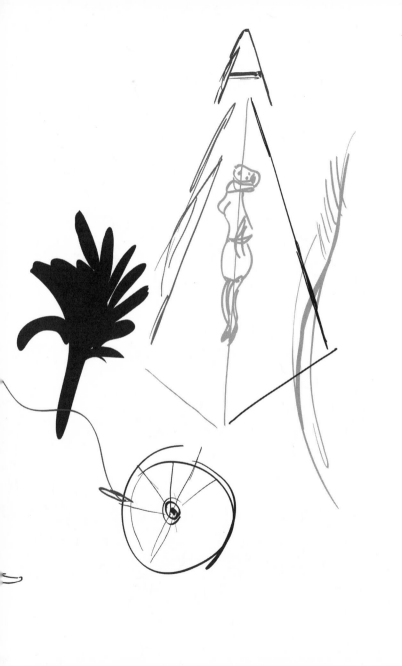

INFINITE RECURSOR OR THE BRIDE OF DJ SPINOZA

The bride of DJ Spinoza
has an absolute cleavage
like that between natural numbers and Aleph-null

In place of hands
she waves aspirated ands

She dots her eyes
all over her thighs

DJ Spinoza
plays a viola
bump-bump-bumping past her balcony
in a runaway stroller

As MC Squared
fresh from the wash
walks out on the balcony
while eating a brioche

DJ Spinoza grabs his gun
but MC Squared has a bigger one
DJ Spinoza shoots and misses
The bullet falls into a glass of mineral water and hisses

Now MC Squared gets his turn
He looks more stern than a Mesosoic fern
He squeezes the trigger and cries,
    "O gosh! Now I have to wash
again! What a dumb error! I squeezed the brioche!"

And he retires from the theater of operations
frantically sprinkling baby powder on his expiring shirt
The Bride of DJ Spinoza emerges onto the balcony

THE BRIDE OF DJ SPINOZA: Who's that that stalks by the zoccolo
    ЦОКАЯ ВОКРУГ ДА ОКОЛО
    studying me through an ocular
    What an invasive f*** you are

DJ SPINOZA: It's me that stalks by the zoccolo
    ЦОКАЯ ВОКРУГ ДА ОКОЛО
    Come down softly and open your door
    cause I got more rhymes than Joseph Brodsky
      I got more rhymes than Leon Trotsky
        Brodsky
                  Trotsky
          Brodsky
                  Trotsky
   La-là

She comes down and drop-kicks him in the head.

BRIDE: Eighty-nine, eighty-nine, fifty-two,
         eighty-nine, eighty-nine, fifty-two,
         What am I going to, going to do,
         what am I going to do?
         Nourrice!

Enter Nurse.

NURSE: Oui, madame.

BRIDE: Don't you oui-madame me! Nourrice, j'ai mal!

NURSE: Mâle, madame? Au contraire, vous êtes très féminine.

BRIDE: Sacrebleu! Mal à l'estomac!

NURSE: Je vous apporte la pilule, madame.

BRIDE: Merci, nourrice. Vous êtes très sympa.

Exit Nurse.

BRIDE: I have invented the machine
         for the invention of the machine
         for the invention of the machine
         ...
         for the invention of the machine!

Now
I will go rest on my laurels
asking myself why
O Unnamable One
did you invent this machine?
Because my heart...

Enter Nurse.

NURSE: La pilule, madame.

BRIDE: Merci, nourrice.

Exit Nurse.

BRIDE: Where was I? O yes!
Because my heart... well... whatever.

DJ Spinoza appears at the window.

DJ: Madam, without any words
say yes or no.

BRIDE: I can't.

DJ: X!

BRIDE: X?! Why?

DJ: Z!

BRIDE: Alas! I'm at the end of my alphabet! *(To DJ Spinoza.)*
　　　Okay, you won, I'll marry you.

Rejoicing at the window, DJ Spinoza falls onto the flowerbed and sprains his ankle.

The woodchuck and the woodpecker
met each other in the wood.
The woodchuck and the woodpecker
could not make themselves understood.

The woodchuck and the woodpecker
walked away really bumming.
Alas! No two species of animals
have a language in common.

Enter Andrew Marvell.

MARVELL: I am coming back from Russia where I worked as
　　　secretary to the Earl of Carlisle. My year is 1663-65. The
　　　Russians are utter savages and speak almost no Latin.

Enter Old Believer.

OB:　Guten Tag!

AM:　Salve, viator.

OB: Ich bin...

AM: Aye, I been there myself. *(To Old Believer.)* Cogito ergo sum!

OB: Haben Sie...

AM: Quid?

OB: Ja!

AM: Sic?

OB: Ja!

AM: Sick, O sick! I do not understand his Russian but I think he is asking for money. *(To Old Believer.)* Pecuniam non habeo.

OB: Wie bitte?

AM: Non habeo! Habere! Habeo, habes, habet, habemus, habetis, habent! Pecuniam! Pecunia, pecuniae...

OB: КУКУ ДА КУКУ, НЕ ПОЛОУМЕН ЕСИ? АЛИ ДЫКИЙ? МЕРИКАНЕЦ ПЕРНАТЫЙ, СИТТИНГ СТУЛ? ОТПРЯНУ АЗ ВО ХРИСТЕ, ЗАНЕ УКУСИТ. *(To Andrew Marvell.)* Guten Abend, mein Herr! Auf wiedersehen!

Exit Old Believer.

AM: Foofff! He's gone. And I'm tired. I'll just relax under this three here and see if I can grok me a green thought in a green shade.

Falls asleep. Enter MC Squared.

MC²: The bride of DJ Spinoza
talks on a Motorola.
She's got night-vision goggles,
she rides an Internet crawler.

Her smile has something
rigorously logical,
more topological
than anthropological.

How much do I love her?
Let me count the ways.

Counts. After an hour, Andrew Marvell wakes up.

AM: Boy, that's what I call a snooze! That felt, like, thirty thousand years. Hm, and my pants are stained. *(Sees MC Squared.)* Who's that?

MC²: ...five million and two, five million and three...

AM: Hey! Who are you?

MC²: I am MC Squared.

AM: And I am Andrew Marvell.

BRIDE: *(Opening envelope.)* I can't read this! All the letters are
    upside down. *(Turns the letter over.)* O! My! God!

Enter DJ Spinoza, limping and in headphones.

DJ: *(At the top of his lungs.)* ПУСТЬ ЗАВИСТЬ БЛАГОРОДНАЯ
    ВСКИПАЕТ, КАК ВОЛНА!

BRIDE: DJ, they've disembarked!

DJ: ИДЕТ ВОЙНА НАРОДНАЯ,
    СВЯЩЕННАЯ ВОЙНА!

BRIDE: Hey DJ! Hey DJ! Hey DJ! DJ, they've disembarked!

DJ: Who "they"?

BRIDE: MC Squared and his Latinist!

DJ: MC Squared, that smiling villain,
    why, he's been my nemesis and mimesis,
    my oasis, Osiris and osmosis,
    my peristalsis and pediculosis,
    furunculosis, avitaminosis,
    anamorphosis, osteoporosis,

my apophasis, symbiosis, scoliosis,
ever since I was a young Jedi Knight,
ever since I studied with Mr. Cogito!

BRIDE: We must meet them in combat.

ACT FOUR

MC²: Now, let's see...
I got my halberd, I got my harquebus,
I got my whatchammacallit—morning glory? No.
Morning worry? No. Morning sorry? No.
Morning star!
In short I'm dressed cap à pie
and I don't even have to polish my armor
because I rented a page. Hey page!

Enter Page.

MC²: Page, why so blank? Heh heh heh...

PAGE: I'm thinking, my lord.

MC²: Thinking? No thinking on the job, do you hear? Go see
how Captain Marvell is doing. Oh never mind, there's the
man himself.

Enter Andrew Marvell with troops.

AM: Troops,
        make loops!

The troops walk around in circles.

AM: They're battle-ready, my lord!

Enter DJ Spinoza, the Bride of DJ Spinoza and their troops.

DJ: Troops,
        take poops!

The troops...

DJ: They're battle-ready, madam!

BRIDE, MC², DJ *and* AM: Attack!

TROOPS: URRRAAAAAAAAAAAAAAAAAAAAAAAAAAAAAA
        AAAA!!! *(Exit fighting.)*

Then Andrew Marvell says to DJ Spinoza, "DJ! I found a
    grammatical error in your *Ethics*!"
And DJ Spinoza replies, "Captain Marvell! You don't got poetics,
    you got pathetics!"
Andrew Marvell takes a running start and tries to drive a stake
    through DJ Spinoza's heart,
But the DJ deflects the stake to a steak and follows it with a tart.
Then DJ Spinoza throws *frutti di mare* all over the metaphysical
    poet

Who stands there with octopus in his wig, scallops in his beard,
  and jumbo shrimps peering out of the pockets of his coat,
But does he care? No! The food fight acquires more vehemence,
Andrew Marvell pelts DJ Spinoza with ketchup packets and
  after-dinner mints.
How the ketchup packets explode! But the DJ has his own
  artillery
He delivers a volley of beef liver against Andrew Marvell's
  showy livery.
Roast chicken fly, some with skewers still lodged in their gullets,
Polenta mortars go off and whistle the caper-bullets,
Pad Thai emplacements drown in sauce hollandaise
Yet still the opponents struggle, slipping in mayonnaise,
Until, ricocheting off shields of pizza, a spinning samosa
Savagely tenderizes the unfortunate DJ Spinoza.
He blinks several times, absurdly clutching a chicken gizzard,
Then falls to the ground like a Soviet-bloc tower of Pisa,
Andrew Marvell is victorious.

Exit Andrew Marvell picking strands of spaghetti off his coat.

MC²: Pretty good fight, eh? I kept waiting for them to bring out
  the huevos rancheros.

BRIDE: DJ! DJ! Alas, he's stiffening. *(Weeps.)*

MC²: Never mind him—you can have me instead. I love you,
  you know. We make a nice couple.

BRIDE: Leave me alone.

MC²: But I won!

BRIDE: Och! You are so shallow. What do you know of love? All you can think about is yourself. You are such a... man! What can you possibly know of love? Love has to do with other people. (*Sings.*)

> Volevo essere la sposa
> del famoso
> > DJ Spinoza,
> Volevo essere la sposa
> del famoso
> > DJ Spinoza...

TUTTI (*including troops of both sides, suddenly appearing and just as suddenly disappearing*): Fu Spinoza, il DJ! Fu Spinoza, il—

MC²: Cause I was born to be ill
> > to a quail for a quill,
> I brush my grill with an electric drill
> > and I don't even pay the eclectic bill!

Any MC's in the house? You ain't nothing before me! You suck!

> This one MC came up to me,
> He said, Why you don't take me seriously?
> I said, I don't take you seriously
> cause you got four eyes like Brenda Lee.

He said, Who's Brenda Lee? You use her for the rhyme!
I said, I use her for the rhyme?
He said, You use her for the rhyme.
I said, Shut up and listen, you talking mime,
Cause I rock the mic like tequila rocks lime!

I rock the mic like tequila rocks lime!
Do you rock the mic like tequila rocks lime?
You don't rock the mic like tequila rocks lime.
So shut up and let me improve your mind!

My various peeps are no Little Bo Peeps,
They ride in jeeps with automatic clips.
When I walk in the room, it's a total eclipse:
The ladies scream, O my God, check out those hips!
I say, Hey ladies, you got the time?
Cause I rock the mic like tequila rocks lime!

*He remains standing alone onstage. Efficient pause. Enter Andrew
Marvell in a fresh change of clothes, leading the Bride of DJ Spinoza
prisoner.*

MC²: Captain Marvell, you fully deserve a medal for your
       exploits!

AM: My lord, your troops
       are scattered and the enemy
       is also scattered.
       They flee each other through the bogs and swamps,
       each man atremble like a hind,

and so frequently do they turn to check what's behind them, that many have run into trees and gotten grievously hurt.

MC²: You lost my army!

AM: I caught your bride!

BRIDE: I ran into a tree!

MC²: You lost my army! Walrus, give me back my legions!

AM: Your allusion is to Varrus, not walrus. There's no *l* and the first letter is a *v* not a *w*.

MC²: W?! I'll quadruple you, I'll octuple you, I'll topple you, stomp on you, crumple you!

AM: All of that? Why, you... No more of this you-business with you! Thou art a nincompoop and a chump! A rear admiral, thou art admirable from the rear but thy front is a spitting image, thou purple-assed baboon!

MC²: I'll teach you common usage, you action figure!

They run at each other. The Bride of DJ Spinoza makes a dash for it again.

MC², AM: Catch her, catch her! (*Exit running.*)

NURSE: *(In headphones.)* На нас на всех нужна одна победа!
Мы за ценой не постоим!

BRIDE: Put those down. Laissez, laissez. They are still warm.

NURSE: Ô madame, excusez-moi.

BRIDE: Are the contractors here?

NURSE: Oui, madame.

Exit Nurse.

BRIDE: We shall have our day yet, my poor DJ. *(Sings.)*

We were once   making plans   to get married,
Now you lie   all alone   and unburied.
We were one,   now I'm none,   and a nun I shall
always be,

But vengeance belongs,
vengeance belongs,
vengeance belongs
TO ME!

When we danced   we conversed   of the future.
Could we've known   that it harbored   a butcher?
Now I cry   and I weep   and I'm plunged
into deep ennui,

But vengeance belongs,
           vengeance belongs,
                       vengeance belongs
       TO ME!

Now those fops triumph, but it'll be vice versa
when I bring out my INFINITE RECURSOR.

ACT FIVE, SCENE 2

AM: My lord, I must to England. I got a friend there who's
      writing a long poem. He thinks he can justify the ways of
      God to man. I'm like, Milton, it won't work, you're better
      off in the Catskills.

MC²: I am sad to see you go. It's been a pleasure having you
      here.

AM: The pleasure is all mine.

MC²: No, I mean it. A real pleasure.

AM: And I mean it. Pleasure all mine. All of it.

MC²: How can it all be yours if some of it is mine?

AM: Are you starting again?

MC²: I starting again?

They run at each other. Crash. The Bride of DJ Spinoza drives a Supersized Machine onto the stage.

BRIDE: You're finished, dyspeptic duo! I'm gonna freeze-dry the both of you with my Infinite Recursor!

MC², AM: What's an infinite recursor?!

BRIDE: It's a machine that generates infinite processes. If I point it at you all your processes will become infinite.

MC², AM: You mean we'll live forever?!

BRIDE: No, I mean instant and simultaneous failure of all bodily functions. Ha ha ha. And FYI—I designed it myself! All it's made of are some logical symbols, some operators and a whole lot of scrap iron. Ha ha ha. Vengeance is mine! Ready, set... freeze!

MC Squared and Andrew Marvell tumble.

MC²: *(Raising his head.)* Am I dead?

AM: *(Examining his clothes.)* Have I bled?

BRIDE: *(Jumps down.)* Oh no! It applied itself to itself first! *(Kicks it.)* Stupid first-generation device!

MC², AM: *(Approaching with swords drawn.)* You should have tested it. You should have freeze-dried a cat or something.

BRIDE: I'm not an engineer, I'm a mathematician. I'm not even an applied mathematician, I'm pure.

MC², AM: You won't be so pure when we get through with you!

Enter DJ Spinoza.

BRIDE, MC², AM: DJ Spinoza!

DJ: I knew you were gonna say that!

AM: He rose from the dead, AAAAAAAAAAAAAAAAAA AAAAAAAAAAAAAAAAAAAAAAAAAAAAAAAAAA !!! *(Exit running.)*

MC²: I'll fight you to the death, fearsome specter,
even if that death is my own. Engage.

DJ: With pleasure, MC Squared. Or is the pleasure
all yours?

DJ Spinoza and MC Squared
now meet upon the lea.
If you want to know what happened,
endure the poetry.

The DJ is a DJ,
the MC an MC.
There's so much vinyl in the air,
that neither of them can see.

Technology is the Queen of War,
than Brothers Grimm she's more grim.
DJ Spinoza launches
a new software program.
The program deals the MC
a memorable pogrom.

MC Squared is wounded. A grimace of pain crosses his face. The trees
stand there, looking on. The woodchuck and the woodpecker stand there,
looking on. They have no face. He falls.

The DJ is upon him
with murder in his eyes,
but when his glasses slip off the bridge of his nose,
the murder leaves his eyes.

 "Alas, where are my glasses?"
the DJ screams and shouts.
"Surrender," says the MC,
"or I'll knock the lenses out."

"O do not touch my lenses,"
the DJ cajoles and begs.
"Surrender," says the MC,
"or I'll tear off your legs."

The MC feels his shoulder tapped,
the Bride delivers a punch.
The MC quickly crumples
and shows everybody his lunch.

The MC undulates like a worm, choking on his own blood and vomit.
This brings up several issues. Why do we inflict pain on those who feel
it as acutely as we do? Is it because we can't be bothered to translate
ourselves into the mind of another? Is laziness of imagination the root
of evil? Is art then a way to fight evil? But what art, how to find that art,
how to find that word which isn't purchased with somebody else's pain?

DJ SPINOZA: *(Finding his glasses.)* I can see again!

BRIDE: O marvelous specter, have you come
        to save me or to haunt me? Leave. Your face
        reminds me of the happiness I had
        and shall no more. Have pity, go. Yet stay,
        sweet specter.

DJ: Specter? I'm as alive as the next guy. In fact, I am more
        alive then the next guy.

BRIDE: Prove it.

DJ: Will this narrative be enough? I came to at night under
        a pile of corpses. There were elbows in my mouth, knees
        in my ribs and heads in my groin. It was our troops.
        Here and there I recognized a familiar face.

I lay there pinned down, waiting to be removed by the
  bulldozer,
the bulldozer that comes in such instances always,
pushing a mountain of heads and limbs
into the yawning earth, to conceal, to say, "There's no
  mass grave here,
nothing happened, you might as well plant, eat, copulate,
nothing happened here, but they grow well, the cereals,
  don't they?"
So I lay there. But when in the distance I heard the roar of
  the bulldozer
before the first signs of dawn broke, in the emptiest hour,
the hour when herds of bulldozers
come out and spread over the face of the earth with their
  blades lowered,
I gathered all my strength together and cried, "No way,
  man! You're DJ Spinoza,
don't think of these corpses as corpses—think of them as
  poets waiting to read at an open mic—"
Poets? I hadn't thought poetry had undone so many!
I'll chew my way to the exit! This kike is taking a hike!
So here I am.

BRIDE: O DJ, I can't believe it, you're alive.
  Let's get married immediately!

DJ: Married immediately?
      But I'm only thirty-five!

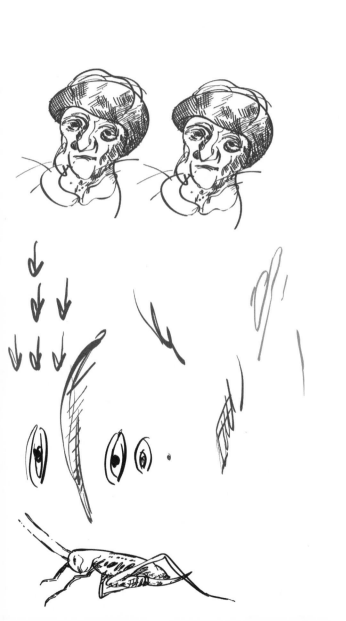

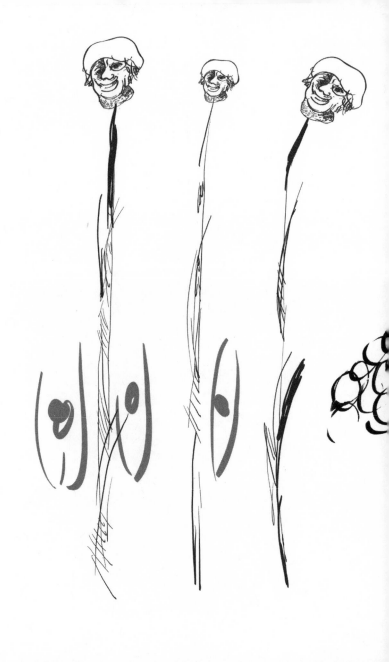

DJ SPINOZA DOES NOT FIGHT THE BEGRIFFON

1.

Excuse me, is this P or ¬P, the sky or not the sky, the building or
	not the building?
Does the building imply the sky, does the sky imply the building,
what does the not-building imply?

There are waves to one side of the building
	and a boat.
We stepped down into the boat
	and sailed away.

We sailed past an island where Dave Cameron stood
	reading his poetry.
We sailed past an island where Brandon Downing stood
	reading his poetry.
We sailed past an island where Macgregor Card stood
	reading his poetry.

So much poetry for one day!

2.

SOME QUESTIONS:

Are there books in the building? Is there a book on fire
	in the building?
Is there a book on fire in a book on fire in the building?
Is this the beginning of number?

SOME ANSWERS:

The beginning of number is song. The song
is not about anything. It gave birth to the world.
The world is not about anything.

SOME COMMENTS:

Animals gather around the song. They listen, tilting
    their heads.
They have large eyes. We can count the animals.

3.

"What do we do when the song ends for somebody
    what do we do
Do we say, Don't go
    what will I do if you do
Do we run to the doctor and cry,
    Give me an MRI, doctor! What he has
I might have it too
    Do we lie around despondent and blue
O why do you go, why do you go
    There's so little time left

"Let us sit down, me and you
    Let me help you sit down
because I am now a man and for you
    it's hard even to sit down
What do we do now, what do we do
    Let us speak, me and you

We never learned to speak, me and you
   Let us start, ma-ma da-da
You say *The Metamorphosis*
   is about dying
Let us sit on this rock, me and you
   I say, ma-ma da-da
We live in Brooklyn
   We have a dog"

This is the song as heard / unheard by the animals. By some of
   the animals. By none of the animals. There are no animals.

There are only points, each at the convergence of an infinity
   of structures. The structures appear to be of metal. They
   oscillate. They make noise.

4.

What is mathematics to animals? Is P or ¬P true
for all animals? Does 1+1=2
for all animals? Is there a me and you
for all animals? What is

mathematics to animals? What are animals
to mathematics? Take away mathematics
and there are no animals. Take away animals
and there is no mathematics.

The animals gather for a concert of mathematics. We sail
   past them.
They are capable of love. We sail past them.

5.
We sail and we repeat. What do we repeat? Words.
What are these words? There is a word for sky
and there is a word for building.

What do they mean? They mean sky
and building. The sky is blue.
The building is white and pink.

DJ Spinoza
is a mighty wrestler

His angel is a book
He dreams he climbs

lines of print
He shall be a father

of notions
O DJ Spinoza

dandruff speckles
your gaberdine

Your wife squints
as if threading a needle

Behind your house
your children torture a cat

Nations shall cast off your yoke
after murderous convulsions

Your streets shall fill
with confusion of faces

Your synagogues shall convert
to movie theaters and swimming pools

You shall be replaced
with the silicon chip

since you are both so small
and so black

When his father lay dying
DJ Spinoza knelt before him in goatskins
and pretended he was someone else.

Cropdusters buzzed over the cornfields,
the knocking of washing machines was heard throughout the land
and the olive trees produced olives with newfound, masculine
    power.

Poor father! He was becoming smaller,
growing waxier and more inaccessible.
His face bore the stamp of chemotherapy.

He made efforts to speak, but the words shattered
into letters stamped on white plastic blocks in the game of Boggle
The family bent forward to see what he was saying.

It was, *"màmochka, màmochka."*
DJ Spinoza unwittingly looked at his own mother,
who sat as close to the bed as she could, grasping his father's hand.

Now the Lord said to DJ Spinoza,
Get out of your country!

And DJ Spinoza said to the Lord,
What country are you talking about, Lord?

And the Lord said to DJ Spinoza,
Good start, good start, for I shall make you lost among nations.

And DJ Spinoza said to the Lord,
Make me lost among nations, Lord, for I am already lost
    among myself.

And the Lord said to DJ Spinoza,
Why do you bring up personal problems? Hire a therapist—
    you who made the schools ring with *Sic probo*!

And DJ Spinoza said to the Lord,
Lord, is not the set of things in your apprehension infinite?

And the Lord said to DJ Spinoza,
All things are one thing but the irrationals are something else.
    Haven't you heard of the diagonal proof?

And DJ Spinoza said to the Lord,
So there is another God above you?

And the Lord said to DJ Spinoza,
Read my lips: get out of your country!

And DJ Spinoza said to the Lord,
But surely just the fact that you're talking in language means
you admit of emotions.

And the Lord said to DJ Spinoza,
Do you want to be numbered on the tip of my boot?

And DJ Spinoza made himself scarce. He lived among the deaf
and became as one blind. He lived among the blind and
became as one deaf. He saw never the sea. He awoke in a
room with four walls.

The room moved. He heard the voice of a child but what it
said he ignored. He awoke from awaking. He was aged,
wrinkled, hairless, toothless. He remembered nothing of
what had happened to him.

Said DJ SPINOZA to his friend MC SQUARED:

> Let us go slay the Begriffon!
> Frightful is the Begriffon and sharp are his claws,
> He disobeys rules and cares nothing for laws,
> He is full of effects but do they have a cause?
> Let us go slay the Begriffon!

Said MC SQUARED to his friend DJ SPINOZA:

> Why should we add to the misery of the world?
> Even the wicked have feelings!
> They shout and they quarrel
> Cause they're anal and oral,
> Problems make them immoral—
> They're wicked *because* they have feelings!

DJ SPINOZA:

> Well, what do you want to do then?
> Do you want to watch TV? No!
> Do you want to play cards? No!
> Do you want to go get a beer? "I'm sick of beer, it's so
>   fattening!"
> Let us go slay the Begriffon!

MC SQUARED:

Are you always so restless because you're reckless
Or are you so reckless because you are restless?
Can't you even for a moment
Think of how it'll make you feel in the morning?
Tell me you won't be a) whining; b) kvetching;
    c) moaning!
And besides—even the wicked have feelings!

So the two friends went off to slay the Begriffon. But when they were halfway to the House of Mostly Unlike, DJ Spinoza realized he forgot his sword at home—and you can't slay the Begriffon with no sword! They had to return for the sword but by the time they did, it was already too late to do anything. They put slaying the Begriffon off for tomorrow and went to sleep extremely content with themselves.

I.

When the Bride of DJ Spinoza lay in the arms of MC Squared,
DJ Spinoza became bitter indeed

What are you doing,
he said, don't I have arms?

Yes, she said, but his are different
For example, you don't wear the same watch
And he respects me
whereas you, well, you are you

2.

DJ Spinoza does not know what to do with love
It's hard to be in love
and a solipsist at the same time

My beloved, he says, left me
for her vineyard I hadn't kept

The Eden is as it was, the Eve is as she was
but the Adam is different
and soon I too will lie next to somebody else
at once diffident and indifferent

Man! says God
What is it with you philosophers?
Is it because you're always asking why
that it just automatically segues into whining?

Okay, says DJ Spinoza
wiping tears away with the back of his hand
But if we don't talk about my problems, what are we going to
    talk about?

3.
DJ Spinoza excelled at philosophy
but philosophy is not wisdom.

He drew up propositions,
made astonishing distinctions,
denied origin, effected *epochē*:
Why was he still so unhappy?

Wisdom is knowing how to love,
DJ Spinoza, it is an action,
dogs have it
more than you do.

A portrait of MC Squared
in fluted armor
with a yellow ribbon around the codpiece.

A portrait of DJ Spinoza
among pillows and coffee cups:
MY BROTHER WENT TO MECCA
AND ALL I GOT WAS THIS LOUSY TURBAN.

A set of galleys
with lots of errors.

Our goal, as we move into the future,
is to try to achieve the same level of cleanliness,
tidiness and lack of clutter that we were capable of achieving
    this week.

At the end of_____
stands a pavilion. DJ Spinoza
inhibits it. His sword
is a spade, he tries not to think about needles
            because he is afraid of scratching, his boats
are vermilion.

He walks to the right and starts a song,
he walks to the left and tells a tale.

Sometimes MC Squared comes by
and they discuss slaying the Begriffon.

The mathematical project is over
and the criterion for truth is gone.

There's only language
in which you can say anything,

the brief and tedious kick called life
with which you don't quite know what to do.

Maybe it's time for you to teach literature—
            These are some excerpts
            from their conversations.

They stroll downwind from the polygon,
past those whose eyes have overgrown with meat,
who squat, fingers writhing
slogans on dust: THE BLIND ARE BETTER
THAN THE DEAF! MUCH BETTER! AND HOW!
WHAT PART OF THIS
DON'T YOU UNDERSTAND?

When they reach the beginning of_____
they turn around and return

talking of love as concept and practice
and how it's so much easier as a concept.

I know what you mean, he says,
                    I tried to add one and one
but the result isn't what it used to be.

Why don't we be friends, what is it like
being friends,

friends stand up for each other, with friends
you are not alone.

Now the Lord God said to DJ Spinoza,
  Baruch, are you there?

And DJ Spinoza replied to the Lord God,
  Here I am!

GOD: Baruch, how about you be my mirror?

DJ: Mirror? But *God* spelled backwards reads *dog*!

GOD: Don't be so literal.
  Tell me something nice
  about myself, tell me I exist.

DJ: You exist.

GOD: No, say it like you mean it.

DJ: Why are you so needy today? Is everything alright?

GOD: I was just thinking: If I really am Absolutely Transcendent,
  then I don't exist at all, do I?

DJ: But, Lord, remember the *cogito*: If you think you don't
  exist, you exist!

GOD: Yeah, I guess so.

Silence.

Now the Lord God said to DJ Spinoza,
> Baruch!

And DJ Spinoza replied to the Lord God,
> Here I am!

GOD: Are you sure? I mean, your argument, it's not just verbal, is it? Does it really apply?

DJ: Inasmuch as anything applies.

GOD: But nothing *really* applies. Does the word *dog* apply to dogs? Ask yourself that.

DJ: Does the word *dog* apply to dogs?

GOD: Nu?

DJ: I can't tell. Shall we test it? *(DJ Spinoza walks over to Yasha.)* Yasha! Yasha! *(Yasha wakes up.)* Yasha, dog! Dog, Yasha! Dog, Yasha, dog! *(Yasha stares incomprehendingly.)*

GOD: You see?

Waalking through the forest one day MC Squared met the philosopher Kierkegaard.

KIERKEGAARD: If P, you will regret it.
        If ¬P, you will also regret it.
        P or ¬P, you will regret either.
        P and ¬P can't be, and so you will regret it all the more!

MC²: Why so sore, N?

KIERKEGAARD: I need to beat somebody up. *En garde!*

MC²: You'll regret it.

KIERKEGAARD: Ach, what won't I regret.

They fight. Kierkegaard is wounded. MC Squared readies a coup de grâce.

GOD: Stop! Stop! (*Sings.*)
        It is wrong
                    to commit
                                violence!

MC²: But I'm strong!

KIERKEGAARD: But I submit!

GOD: Get your eye a lens!

MC² *and* KIERKEGAARD: Huh?

GOD: *(Aside.)* It is rhyme
                  that hath made me
                             obscure:
Human language
           is sick
                    beyond cure!
(To them.)
           Get a lens
                  if your eye
                         cannot see.

MC² *and* KIERKEGAARD: *(Putting in lenses.)*
           Now I see
                  I'm like you,
                        you're like me!

They embrace. The End.

for Sonya

This is my main hand,
says the Pirate,

and it has made me what I am: the main man
on the Main!

Yes, I'm a radical rapscallion
cruising around in my Spanish galleon,

filling the sails with northeasterly trade winds,
discharging cannons and making nice with the maidens.

I stand on the fore, I stand on the aft,
it's the lifestyle I like, not the golden calf.

Any time you ask me if I want rum,
I'll say, Thank you, I will have some!

Enter MC Squared.

MC²: Ahoy mate,
           spare some pieces of eight?

PIRATE: Get a job, you nogoodnik!

MC²: Alas, I am psychologically unable to work.

PIRATE: I can identify with that.

Offers to give him a coin but MC Squared catches him by the arm and performs jewjitsu.

MC²: Pirate pirate, tell me the value of pi!

PIRATE: 3.14156...—I don't know how it ends!

MC²: Then prepare to die!

PIRATE: Ack! Spare me please! Don't orphan my parrot!
I'll give you a diamond of 25 carat.

MC²: Save you carrots for bunnies! They'll clean 'em and
clear 'em.
Gimme the proof of the Pythagorean theorem!

PIRATE: No!!! That's the theorem before which I in fear am!
Please mister,

> Ask me something I'm good in,
> like romance or dance.
> When this leg wasn't wooden
> how I pranced without pants!
>
> When we pull into port
> I rush off to ballet,
> greeting every *plié*
> with a loud *Olé!*

MC²: Well then who in the Bay Area is the famousest dancer on *pointe*?

PIRATE: That's easy! It's Sonya Ostashevskaya-Gohstand.

MC²: You are free to go.

The pirate gets up, groaning and rubbing his ПОЯСНИЦА. *Curtain.*

A is for Axiom
that proved arbitrary.

B is for Binomial
whose terms never vary.

C is for Circumference
that goes around and around.

D is for Derivative
left to lie on the ground.

E is for e
(tautologically shown).

F is for Frustrum,
a beheaded cone.

G is for Games
in which all players lose.

H is for Horror
of the Hypotenuse.

I is for Identity,
when A=A.

What J is for,
I just cannot say.

K is another
katatonic letter.

L is the Lowest
common denominator.

M is for Moebius
whose head was all face.

N stands for Number
in the general case.

O is for "Oops,
I'm dividing by zero!"

P: Proposition
for which slapped was the hero.

Q is for Quotient:
"You guys smoked all the dope!"

R is Remainder
or so we hope.

S is for Sine curve
that reclines in the nude.

T is for Tangent,
absconding for good.

U is for Union
(what else could it be?).

V is for Venn diagram
which joins two, or three.

W is for Whole
that equals its part.

X is a variable
made up by Descartes.

Y is also a variable,
it transforms on the go.

Z is for Zero,
sometimes written as O.

What do you think, says DJ Spinoza,
am I free?

You are free
if you think you are free,
    says God.

Do you think I am free to think so?
    says DJ Spinoza.

Are you trying to do an infinite regress?
    says God.

No, I mean it,
    says DJ Spinoza.

You are free to think so
and you are free when you think so,
    says God.

And what happens when I am not thinking I am free?
    says DJ Spinoza.

Then you aren't,
    says God.

What do you want me to do, says DJ Spinoza,
walk around, going "I'm free, I'm free, I'm free?" I can't think
    anything else?

You can, says God.
It's just that your other thoughts have to be built on it.

How do you build a thought on a thought?
    says DJ Spinoza.

In the same way as the sum of angles in a triangle being 180°
follows from the idea of triangle,
    says God.

That's beautiful, says DJ Spinoza.
But is beauty an indication of truth?

Is beauty an indication of truth?
    says DJ Spinoza.

Take P=P, says God.
It's beautiful and it's true.

Examples are not proofs,
    says DJ Spinoza.

What kind of proof do you want then?
    says God.

A convincing one,
    says DJ Spinoza.

Isn't the beautiful convincing? says God.
When we love we aren't convinced that we love?

No,
    says DJ Spinoza.

No?
    says God (in amazement).

We can love without knowing we love, says DJ Spinoza.
Sometimes we know afterwards. Sometimes we never know at all.

What are you—French? says God.
How would you know you loved when you don't know you
loved?

I don't know,
    says DJ Spinoza.

Let's return to "Sometimes we know afterwards," says God.
Still, we know.

But do we know that it's true what we know?
    says DJ Spinoza.

Well, *I* know, says God.
I am God.

Look at you, says DJ Spinoza. You're a singularity!
I'm not talking about singularities, I'm talking about us.

But I am among the us, says God.
Excuse *me,* here I was, thinking I was among the us!

Are you being difficult? says DJ Spinoza.
Because if you are being difficult, we can stop right here and now.

I am being difficult? says God.
I have a right to my own identity!

Okay, okay,
    says DJ Spinoza.

Okay then,
　　says God.

Where were we?
　　says DJ Spinoza.

Is conviction an indication of truth?
　　says God.

Are you there, God?
It's me, DJ Spinoza.
How are you doing today—
okay?
What? You don't exist?
Are you depressed again?
Who am I talking to, then?
Who?! What number is this?
The number of what? Sorry,
can you speak louder,
you got some kind of screaming going on in the background—
Hello?

Hangs up the phone.

What was that?! "The Number of the Yeast"?
Sounds like an all-girl metal band from Scandinavia.

Dials.

Hi, is this God?
It's me, DJ Spinoza.
Nice to hear you, too.
Hey, I wrote a new poem
And I want to share it with you!
What do you mean you already heard one today
and that's plenty? What kind of explanation

is that? Who called you, anyway?
Morris Imposternak? That fake Russian poet?
Like, he read you from his book,
My Third Cousin Twice Removed—Life? Man, that guy!
I saw him in a coffeehouse this morning,
trying to attract girls by looking pensive.
Hey, do you mind calling me back, this is kind of expensive?
Hello?

He sits down. Nothing happens. The poem ends.

DJ Spinoza is shewn
as a thing of n heads

He rewrites and he rewrites
he rewrongs

Zum Beispiel:

What have I done to my world
It had an *l* in it

Now I sit in this poem
with no place to go!

Excuse me, are these letters or ladders
I shall discard them after use, as the instructions indicated

I climbed to the apex of the haystack although I'm allergic to
    hay and any kind of height makes me nauseated
but the apex of the haystack was identical with the base of the
    haystack

Is there a beginning that is not also an end?
Twenty-three years of school and I don't even know whether
    "this is my foot" is a true statement

If I could write a poem about my intercourse with the world,
it would go like this: Huh?!

Or this:
>I pick up a teacup
>over and over, I cannot stop

>I look at it from the bottom
>I look at it from the top

>I map
>I trap

>What is this thing that answers to the word *cup*
>It doesn't answer

Let us list what we've learned so far:
The color of the sky cannot be named

Having been in love perhaps alters the way you walk or perhaps
>it doesn't
2+2=4 is also in a way an emotion, this is impossible

Ramat, I promised to write you a letter
I write you the wonderful letter *l*

Use it wisely
It does well in all sorts of statements

We have the Phoenicians to thank for it
Think of me as you do

> Excuse me is this a dictionary
> or a fictionary, dysfunctionary
>
> or correctionary, visionary
> or distractionary
>
> Excuse me are these vowels or howls
> Are they our howls, they are so distant

We speak in circles, I teach the *Odyssey*, it is 2004
What kind of philosophy do you want to do, I don't know, what
    kind of philosophy do *you* want to do

I need to say something true but before that I need to say
    something true
What are the conditions of truth, can a proposition end with a
    preposition

Why are you talking to yourself, isn't talking meant for another,
    but I is, yeah you 'is' alright
Let A equal A and ¬A, let it equal B and ¬B, several animals
    walk on grass

The sign says *Don't walk on grass,* but they still walk on grass
    because they don't know how to read
We know how to read, we walk on grass for other reasons

Imagine a language
that is like the world

It is not like anything
that is like language

∞ ∞ ∞

Music swells up
composed of violins

It seems to be true
It is not verifiable

O music that ends
Each thing is an axiom

My shoulder is an axiom
and my hand, my foot

This glass, this table
this wall

There are so many axioms
There is not a single proof

THE PEEPEESAURUS SERIES

for Zaheer

Twenty-seven philosophers
study the eclipse
Twenty-seven philosophers
are made up mostly of lips
Thirteen philosophers on each side
and the center one flips

Says the center philosopher,
You guys are upside down
The other philosophers say,
No, it's you who's upside down
Peepeesaurus comes in and says,
The upside-down is upside down

Have you heard about Peepeesaurus?
He buy a blue balloon
Green is the color of his orange hair
His smile is like a spoon
Yup, when the Peepeesaurus comes
all the philosophers swoon

Says the green philosopher to the orange philosopher,
If N is O then O is P and P is Q
Says the orange philosopher to the lilac philosopher,
I follow you
Says the lilac philosopher to the vermilion philosopher,
What is the color of white?

Says the vermilion philosopher to the egg-yolk-yellow
     philosopher,
Have you heard about the Peepeesaurus?

It's the end of the world. Everybody's expecting the
     Peepeesaurus. Peepeesaurus comes in and says, I'm not
     late, am I?—No, says everybody.

Peepeesaurus Peepeesaurus
Go and make some pee-pee
Peepeesaurus Peepeesaurus
Go and make some pee-pee
Make some pee-pee, Peepeesaurus
Pee-pee is yippee

Peepeesaurus Peepeesaurus
Whatcha doing uptown?
Peepeesaurus Peepeesaurus
You chasing our women around?
Don't you worry, forget your *tzores*
Peepeesaurus is passing by—yeah!—Peepeesaurus

Hey Peepeesaurus, where did you get that hat?
Hey Peepeesaurus, are you allergic to the cat?
Hey Peepeesaurus, you dynamic dude
today in a peepeepositive mood
you're looking *Les-Demoiselles-d'Avignon*-good!

"Ooo Peepeesaurus," philosophers say,
"would you mind if we shouted hooray
as you pass, one-way infinite like a ray,
très chic, très cheek, très shock, très très—
Peepeesaurus, yeay! Notnotpeepeesaurus!"

Peepeesaurus, what's your reply?
Peepeesaurus, he ain't two-ply
No word can apply, Peepeesaurus know why
he's just—yeah!—passing by

Spirit of exile, melancholy demon,
Miscount Malatesta
rides on and rides on and rides and rides.
A fair dose of despair
animates his four eyes.
He cannot find rest—so
he shapes his mustache like the Triborough Bridge,
he screws spurs into his orthotics,
he eats everything in the fridge!

Miscount Malatesta
says to Peepeesaurus,
I challenge you to a duel,
this poem isn't big enough for us!

Peepeesaurus replies, Listen
Miscount Malatesta,
you're famous for your scores
on Scholastic Aptitude Tests, but
what good is a brain, if you're an idiot?
I diagnose you for no fee:
Your life is a total catastro-
phe!

Why is it such a catastro-
phe? says Miscount Malatesta.

Well, ask yourself, says Peepeesaurus, am I happy? I mean, do you
    find all this fighting satisfying in a meaningful kind of way?
    Because it seems to take the place of something constructive,
    of something real. You're afraid, aren't you? Afraid of
    commitment, of choosing and striving and failing? Yet who
    isn't? However, other people manage their fear, whereas
    you—you're so afraid of fear that you've let it steal your life;
    you've accepted an imago of life, a life by default! Wake up!
    It's not like you'll ever be able to do anything over again!

Miscount Malatesta
rides away downcaster and downcaster.

Peepeesaurus
smiles.

....
....
....

Miscount Malatesta
comes upon a philosopher.
The philosopher contemplates
a statue of a rooster in plaster.

Such is our life, says the philosopher,
                    it's chalky, it's outside us,
and we don't really know where to put it.

Caramba, what a disaster!
cries Miscount Malatesta.

Miscount Malatesta
gallops away like crazy,
he enters a dark florist,
he comes out clutching a daisy.

Miscount Malatesta
gallops faster and faster.
He comes upon the philosopher
weeping by the rooster in plaster.

This is for you,
says the Miscount.

Thank you, says the philosopher,
I feel better already!

....
....
....

Miscount Malatesta
will never be self-sequestered.
At the end of the spring semester
he plays inaudible music,
inaudible, audible music
on an invisible Stratocaster!

Some of these poems have previously appeared in *Best American Poetry*, *The PIP Gertrude Stein Awards for Innovative Poetry in English*, *Walt Whitman Hom(m)age*, *A Public Space*, *Barrow Street*, *Boston Review*, *Common Knowledge*, *The Germ*, *FailBetter*, *Greetings*, *Jubilat*, *Lungfull!*, *Octopus: A Visual Studies Journal*, *Octopus Magazine*, *Painted Bride Quarterly*, *Rattapallax*, *Respiro*, and *St. Petersburg Review*. Parts of the DJ Spinoza cycle have also come out in three chapbooks: *The Off-Centaur*; *Infinite Recursor Or The Bride of DJ Spinoza*; and *DJ Spinoza's Dozen*. The author wishes to thank his publishers, friends, readers and listeners for their extraordinary indulgence. An especial thanks goes out to Eugene Timerman and Anna Moschovakis.

The first poem in this book was written in 2001; the last, in 2005. Credit for the name MC Squared goes to Christopher Miragliotta; for that of Peepeesaurus, as well as for the repeating phrase in "First Peepeesaurus," to Zaheer Ze'ev Ostashevsky Coovadia. Any resemblance between this book and life is entirely fortuitous.

POETRY BOOKS
Iterature. Ugly Duckling Presse, 2005.

POETRY CHAPBOOKS
Enter Morris Imposternak, Pursued by Ironies. Ugly Duckling Presse, 2008.
DJ Spinoza's Dozen. Octopus Books, 2007.
Infinite Recursor Or The Bride Of DJ Spinoza. Art by Eugene Timerman. Studio
    RADIA & Ugly Duckling Presse, 2006.
The Off-Centaur. Germ Folios, 2002.
The Unraveller Seasons. Art by Eugene Timerman, 2000.
Noughtbooks 1 and *2.* Art by Eugene Timerman, 1998.
Daphne Azak and Apollo. Art by Darin Klein. 1995.
Fish Sticks. Art by Darin Klein, 1995.

TRANSLATIONS
Dmitry Golynko. *As It Turned Out.* Ed. Eugene Ostashevsky. Trans. Eugene
    Ostashevsky, Rebecca Bella and Simona Schneider. Ugly Duckling
    Presse, 2008.
OBERIU: An Anthology of Russian Absurdism, 1926-1941. Texts by Alexander
    Vvedensky, Daniil Kharms, Nikolai Zabolotsky, Nikolai Oleinikov,
    Yakov Druskin and Leonid Lipavsky. Ed. Eugene Ostashevsky. Trans.
    Eugene Ostashevsky and Matvei Yankelevich. Northwestern University
    Press, 2006.